a **small** book
about the **large** ways
of a **powerful** God
taught to a **weak** creature
in his **brief** life
preparing him for an **endless** eternity

12 life lessons we all must learn
bill elliff

a small book about the large ways of a powerful God taught to a weak creature in his brief life preparing him for an endless eternity
By Bill Elliff

Published by TruthINK Publications
6600 Crystal Hill Road
North Little Rock, Arkansas 72118

Cover Design | Keith Runkle
Illustrations | Jennifer Elliff Rogers

ISBN-13: 978-0-9831168-5-1

Printed in the United States of America

the storyline

dedicated to my wife, Holly

the most adventuresome puddle-jumper
I know. I cannot fathom life without her.

this is a very real and very happy book

LIFE IS A SERIES OF PUDDLES. We jump from one to the next, splashing here and there. Early on, each puddle is an adventure. As years progress, they seem more of an inconvenience. But each puddle holds a lesson to be learned and a tale to be told.

Some are shallow and cause not much concern. Others are deep. To wade in is to get very, very wet. Immersed at times. You can even feel like you're drowning.

There are some who choose to avoid puddles at all costs, never wanting the bother. But to those happy ones who follow God, these immersions become life-giving water. The best lessons are there.

And when you have passed through enough puddles with Christ, you feel you have something to tell. Something that might help those who are coming behind. It's not really about you, but about Him. So, you begin to tell your tale.

And this is mine.

Bill Elliff

Little Rock, Arkansas

2018

chapter 1

in which I learned of the

kindness of God

BILL ELLIFF

IT WAS A BROWN, 18-inch bike with balloon tires. The paint was chipped, the fenders bent, but it was mine, passed down from my older brothers. And now ... *it was time!*

The training wheels had been removed and dad was standing behind me on top of the slight hill in Mr. Hicklin's yard. With a gentle push, he let me go. This time, instead of crashing right into the thorn bush on the left, (which I'd done 100 times), a miracle happened! I went right past the bush and found that glorious balance that only a brand-new bike-rider knows.

I went racing down the sidewalk with the wind in my hair. The baseball card we'd clipped by the tire spokes made my beat-up bike sound like a real, live motorcycle. I was flying and free!

the best

My mom and dad knew how to train their four children to raise the sails and catch the wind. They gave a great balance of loving boundaries, but freedom to explore. They knew this began by modeling a bold, but humble life, surrendered and connected to Jesus Christ. And then, by teaching each child how to know Him and follow the wind of His Spirit.

Dad was like an oak. Solid and reliable. Mom, a tender, joyful willow. Early on, my character lessons were taught to me by my mother. How to treat my brothers and sister, how to be honest and kind. I can hear her singing, "Jesus is all the world to me." And He was. Because she loved Jesus, I loved him too. What was not to love about Him?

Later, my preacher-dad would pick up the baton and teach me skills. How to ride a bike, build a wooden sword in the workshop, sing a song, lead music in a church, and, eventually, preach a sermon. My first sermon was at age seven, thundering forth on a small stool with a hapless, imaginary congregation in three chairs. (I have a copy of my single-page notes, entitled, "The Bible is Right!")

The complementing work of my parents was not perfect, but effective. So much so, that all four children wanted to follow in their footsteps.

It took me years to understand His kindness in the gift of my parents and the early years of my childhood. I had no choice in this. It was merely a gift, imparted to me by a gracious Father.

you would think

... that such a raising would produce children that needed no adjustments. But you would be misjudging the human heart. Everyone needs to be transformed from the inside out.

Gently, the precious wind of God's Spirit began to blow over my life, showing me my sin. It was childlike sin, but the indicator of a dark heart nonetheless. I discovered there were things about me I could not fix—even with my best 7-year-old intentions. This was a lesson I would re-visit in ever-expanding ways throughout my life.

One of my parent's greatest acts was to place us in environments where God was strongly heard and deeply felt. So, we were often at my father's church. One night (in a week set aside to pursue God) a preacher named Chester Swor preached the message I needed.

I realized my sin had separated me from the God I had grown to love. Without a miracle, I would not know him in this life or the next.

At home, I asked my mother about these things and she tenderly showed me the way to Christ. We knelt beside a small tan couch and I prayed in faith for Christ to save me.

And He did.

Overnight, everything changed, more than I knew. My heart was full of joy! I had a hunger to read my Bible. I told mom I wanted to "run up and down the street and tell everybody about Jesus." I told two of my friends about Christ, and they came to Him also. It was the happiest of times.

But when the kindness of God our Savior and His love for mankind appeared, He saved us, not on the basis of deeds which we have done in righteousness, but according to His mercy, by the washing of regeneration and renewing by the Holy Spirit, whom He poured out upon us richly through Jesus Christ our Savior.

(Titus 3:4)

---

another kindness

... came a few years later. Our whole family was at the Christian summer camp in Arkansas that my father directed. A masterful preacher, Dr. Jesse Northcutt, was the speaker for all three weeks. Each week he told the story of Absalom, the adventuresome, golden-haired son who later led a rebellion against his gracious father, King David. I was enthralled.

But it was more than the story that drew me from my wooden bench to the front of the tabernacle one night into the arms of my father. It was God's kindness.

In the miraculous way that God speaks to even a 12-year-old heart, God let me know what I was to do for the rest of my life. It was strong and clear. He knew I needed to understand this calling early. He called me to preach His word.

In all the puddles of my walk since, I have never doubted this calling. Another act of kindness.

if you will look around you

... you will see God's kindness everywhere. It is His kindness that is intended to lead you to turn to Him. And once you do, you will discover His kindness in every scene of the common day, if you have eyes to see. Even when it's raining hard and the puddles are deep.

If you are not careful, you can be like the Israelites who "did not understand [God's] wonders" and "did not remember [God's] abundant kindnesses, but rebelled by the Red Sea" (Psalm 106:7). Some people never open their eyes to the gracious goodness of God and live bitter lives. It is our pride that keeps us from seeing the height of our sin and the depth of God's mercy. We deserve nothing, but He has opened a way for us to have everything that matters.

We will never trust someone we do not believe is good. But the more we understand God's kindness, the more it will lead to a life of gratitude and increasing trust. These two attributes should be the hallmarks of the believer's life.

"Surely goodness and lovingkindness shall follow me all the days of my life," David said (Psalm 23). I have had my share of discipline, tests, and trials. But even these have been allowed by love and rescued by Sovereign purpose.

God has been overwhelming in kindness to me since I was a child. And I expect, knowing Him, it will only increase through eternity.

chapter 2

in which I was pulled by the

power of popularity

WE HAD MOVED from Kansas City, Missouri, back to the town of my birth, Little Rock, Arkansas. I was an impressionable young boy of ten and very social. But the kids in my 4th grade class at Brady Elementary were a bit different than my church buddies in the protected environment I had known.

Setting out to make a few friends, I checked one after another off my list because of their foul language. I quickly went through my whole class in search of one I could find as a friend. Standing on a gravel parking lot, I asked the last boy in my class a simple question.

"Billy, do you cuss?" I innocently asked.

"Hell, yes," he replied.

There it was, and in my immature mind I reasoned, "Well, I guess if I'm going to fit in I need to get with the program." Profanity was awkward at first, but easily learned.

And one thing led to many others. For many years. Seven years, to be exact.

it's hard to believe

... if you don't understand the dynamics of belonging. Everyone wants to be loved. I believe this is hard-wired into us by none other than God Himself. This hunger is there to push us to Him.

But there is another player in the equation. The Father-of-All-Lies understands this longing and uses it to his advantage. He whispers to us that this love can only be found in the approval of others. So, we begin to do whatever we think is needed to gain their attention. To be popular. To fit in. To be loved.

We misjudge the power of this desire. Parents don't remember their childhood, when they compromised to be accepted. If they're not careful they can be naïve and non-protective about their children's friendships.

There is a natural sweetness in children. But every kid wants to be like (and be "liked by") the coolest kid in the class. And thus, it begins.

If unchecked, it can go on for years. In fact, some never grow out of this delusion. They go from one relationship to another, compromising continually, giving what they cannot afford to lose, to gain what they will never get.

the tragedy is

... that people are imperfect. They cannot fill this God-sized hole. At best, their human love is limited and even selfish. The endurance of people's attention is short, giving up when it gets difficult, and the quality of their affection can be shallow. People alone cannot know all your needs and give you the depth of love you desire.

If you look here solely, you will be deeply disappointed. You will find yourself feeling unloved and maybe worthless. You will become ensnared to a man-pleasing, man-fearing spirit which can drive you the rest of your life. I've seen men in their 60's still searching. Such a dilemma will take you places you do not want to go.

I lived there for many years in a desire to be known and loved. To be popular. And I did whatever I thought it would take to get there.

the liberating truth

... is that God's love is perfect. He knows our every need and is driven by His Divine love to always seek the good of others.

This love is perfectly unselfish. Because it is God's love, it is an inexhaustible supply. "Who can ever separate us [His adopted children] from the love of God?" Paul said.

John, who was often described as the Apostle that Jesus loved, was set free by this approval. "We have come to **know** and **believe** the love which God has for us," he said, and, "perfect love [God's love] casts out fear" (1 John 4:16,18). John knew it experientially and believed it completely. It engulfed and enlarged him.

When you know this affectionate approval, and believe that God loves you like this, you are fully and eternally free. You have no one to please, but God. You do not worry about what others think, because your fullness does not depend upon their approval.

If we were playing a game of pick-up basketball and the greatest basketball player in history strolled up, we'd immediately let him captain one of the teams and choose his players. If he picked me, I wouldn't care what you thought of my skills—the best had picked me!

He predestined us to adoption as sons through Jesus Christ to Himself, according to the kind intention of His will, to the praise of the glory of His grace, which He freely bestowed on us in the Beloved.

(Ephesians 1:5-6)

If you have come to know Christ, you have been "accepted in the Beloved," as one version translates the verse above. The pull of popularity is powerless, as long as you remember who you are and Whose you are.

But in my earlier years I didn't know this. And I searched. For seven years.

chapter 3

in which I was

set free by the Spirit

THERE COMES A TIME when you get sick of the world. Tired of living for others' approval. Tired of living for yourself alone. Tired of the world's trinkets. It happened for me in high school.

As I splashed around in the world's puddles, my believing heart began to see them for what they were. It was muddy water. If you know Christ, you know better. But by now, I was trapped. Even though I wanted to escape, I found the lure too strong and my will too weak.

Every time I was stirred at some church event or summer camp, I would "re-dedicate" my life. I vowed to try harder. But the more I tried, the more I failed.

One day, for instance, I came up with a genius plan to overcome one habitual issue—my profanity problem. I told a Christian friend to hit me in the arm every time I said a cuss word. Surely this reform would work!

I came home black-and-blue. (True story).

This was curious to me. Why would this self-improvement scheme—and others I devised for other sins—not work? I was doing my best. Trying hard. Looking at Jesus and trying to ask,

"What Would Jesus Do?" and then vainly seeking to replicate His behavior.

God let me go

... in my "Bill-Elliff-Christianized-Self-Help-Plan" for about a year. He had a deep purpose, knowing I needed to understand the absolute futility of human effort alone. He was teaching me a foundational lesson I would never forget.

No one can live the Christian life on their own.

For I know that nothing good dwells in me, that is, in my flesh; for the willing is present in me, but the doing of the good is not. For the good that I want, I do not do, but I practice the very evil that I do not want.

(Romans 7:18-19)

The Apostle Paul had to see it, and so do we. The futility of humanism. I became more and more desperate for God. And, on April 4, 1969, age 17, something wonderful happened.

I came to the end of myself.

Sitting on the second row at Immanuel Baptist Church in Little Rock, Arkansas, with Angel Martinez preaching, I realized I couldn't do it anymore. I was utterly helpless. I knew God had called me to preach and thought, "How can I preach with such sin in my life?" I threw up my hands in desperation.

"Lord, I completely surrender my life to you. If anything good is going to happen through my life, You're going to need to do it, because I can't," I humbly cried.

"Good!" I could almost hear the affirmation from God, with His knowing smile. "You're finally right where I need you to be."

humble confession

I raced home that night, ran through the front door of 21 Lyric Lane, and fell on my knees before my father. My arms were around his legs, wetting his feet with my tears. I was so ashamed of the deceptive life I had lived, but so filled with joy at what happened that night.

Like a dam breaking, a flood of full confession poured out before my parents. Everything came into the light. My wise father encouraged me to take a legal pad and write "Sin List" on the top and simply write down what God brought to my mind that needed to be dealt with, circling the sins that had affected others. It was seven pages long. Front and back.

Search me, O God, and know my heart; try me and know my anxious ways; and see if there be any hurtful way in me; and lead me in the everlasting way.

(Psalm 139:23-24)

Over the next few weeks, several glorious things happened.

First, I began to clear my conscience both vertically and horizontally —with God and those my sins had affected. It took me awhile, but I can close my eyes and remember the last phone call I made.

"Hello, this is Billy. I'm trying to get my life right with God," I said. "And what I did with you was wrong. Would you forgive me?" That's all I said.

Not a single person refused my request. Many asked for my forgiveness also. When I hung up the phone from that final call, my heart exploded in joy. "The roof was off and the walls were down," as Norman Grubb says in his liberating little book, "Continuous Revival." It wasn't that I hadn't sinned, but to the best of my knowledge, there was no one I had sinned against with whom I had not sought to make it right.

Paul said he "exercised" himself to "always maintain a clear conscience both before God and man" (Acts 24:16). Such exercise, needed continually throughout life, is designed to build the spiritual muscle of humility. It helps us remember our frailty and what happens when we choose to ignore the promptings of God's Spirit or illumination of His Word. It tenderizes our heart.

It has been the regular practice of my life since to pause when I sense a pulling away from God and make such a list. It always proves helpful, reminding me of things I have overlooked in the busyness of life.

Draw near to God and He will draw near to you. Cleanse your hands, you sinners; and purify your hearts, you double-minded ... Humble yourselves in the presence of the Lord, and He will exalt you.

(James 4:8-10)

I was making room for God, but the best was to come.

simple abiding

My father, who had a similar spiritual experience in the 1950's, began to feed me books, tapes, and, most importantly, Scripture passages. He exposed me to an entire school of living by the Holy Spirit's power. Jesus' words in John 15 became alive to me.

> *"I am the true vine, and My Father is the vinedresser ... Abide in Me, and I in you. As the branch cannot bear fruit of itself unless it abides in the vine, so neither can you unless you abide in Me. I am the vine, you are the branches; he who abides in Me and I in him, he bears much fruit, for apart from Me you can do nothing." (John 15:1-5)*

"Apart from me you can do nothing" made absolute sense to me! I had lived it for several years. I realized now that Christ was the Vine (the source of all life and power) and that He lived in me! My singular task was to stay in continual communion and fellowship with Him, trusting the Spirit within me to pour His life and power through me.

I understood now what Paul meant when he said he could "do all things through Christ who strengthens me," and that he was crucified with Christ and he no longer lived, but "Christ now lives in me" (Philippians 4:13, Galatians 2:20).

The Spirit of God had come, at my conversion years earlier, to indwell me, never to leave. But now I was realizing, welcoming, and depending on His presence. He became so real, so present to me! I began to talk to Him in prayer and listen to Him through His Word.

The Christian life could be lived—and lived powerfully— by letting Christ live *through* me! My task was to stay in communion with Him, faithfully following the promptings of His Spirit and the illumination of His Word. Other than my conversion, this was to be the single most life-changing revelation of my life.

My father gave me a recorded sermon by Major Ian Thomas in which he quoted a poem by an anonymous author. It summed up this liberating reality in my life.

> *When Jesus died for me on Calvary,*
> *He paid the penalty for all my sin.*
> *He suffered all the pain, my sinful heart to gain;*
> *And now His Spirit witnesses within.*

I'm just a suit of clothes that Jesus wears.

My body is the house in which He lives!

My voice is His to talk, my feet are His to walk.

I'm just a suit of clothes that Jesus wears.

He rose again to bring abundant grace;

To justify before His Father's face.

I live no more, but He lives out His life through me.

I'm just a vessel fashioned by His grace.

As life goes on I care not, come what may;

He carries all my burdens and my cares.

For me the battle's done—for He's the victory won!

I'm just a suit of clothes that Jesus wears!

I was free. As the years have progressed, this experience has not faded, but grown. It is the source of all that I am or hope to be. Every temptation can be met with "Lord, I cannot handle this, but You can!"

Every time I stand to serve or lead or preach my prayer can be, "Lord, I know that I have no ability to do anything good without

You. But You live in me. I surrender afresh my body. Express Yourself through me today! I will gladly follow You."

The explanation of any good through any true believer's life is simple. It is Christ through a willing vessel.

Simply Christ.

chapter 4

in which I discovered the

reality of God's Word

EVERYONE NEEDS A DISCIPLER. Someone who is a few steps ahead who can lovingly show you the way. Besides my parents, my brother, Jim, was God's gift to me in these formative years.

Jim is three years older than I am and had come to the same spiritual experience a year earlier. In fact, God had used him to bring me to surrender. The sibling fights we had before were no longer possible. Jim would just love me when I got mad, which infuriated me. He had discovered the power of God's presence, and I grudgingly noticed the difference.

God had prepared a spiritual partner for me. Jim was hungry, growing, and loved me as only a brother can. After my fresh surrender to Christ's lordship, we began to grow together. But the first thing he taught me was the most life-changing.

reading the Bible

I knew the importance of the Bible, but had no clue of its transforming power. Without knowing the full reasons why, Jim and I began to read the Bible voraciously. We tried different plans—once reading through the entire Bible in 49 days. (This was incredibly helpful to see the whole scope of the Scripture, and has become a periodic experience for me to this day.) I discovered that a set plan, set place, and set time for the Word and prayer would serve me well the rest of my life.

Jim has always been an innovator. A "trier-of-new-things" to see if they could help him and others. One day he had a new idea.

"Let's put a number in the margin of our Bible when we see something important and then write in our journals that number and the Scripture reference and write down what we see." Quite a challenge.

Little did I know that 50 years later I would still be recording what God said to me through His word, every day. To journal what you are learning is not only a way to write your own commentary on the Scriptures. It is also the fastest way to enhance retention of what God is saying to you. To weave it into the tapestry of your life. And also, to have it handy to share with others.

Before long, I began to realize that the Bible is not only perfectly accurate, it is alive.

> *For the word of God is living and active and sharper than any two-edged sword, and piercing as far as the division of soul and spirit, of both joints and marrow, and able to judge the thoughts and intentions of the heart.*
>
> *(Hebrews 4:12)*

If God is God, you would assume that He would devise a way to commune with His creatures. And He has. He speaks through creation, through our conscience, through His Word by His Spirit, and, most beautifully, through the incarnate Christ.

The Word of God is God, just as much as your word is you. But His Word has an inherent, Divine power like no other book. The Spirit of God can make the Bible come alive to you, communicating it to your heart. His means of speaking directly to you every day!

The Bible is not merely there to enlarge our minds, but to fill our heart as we meet Christ there, listening to His voice. J. C. MacCauley prayed that God would ...

Teach my heart, set free from human forms,
The holy art of reading Thee in every line—

In precept, prophecy and sign;

Till all my vision filled with Thee,

Thy likeness would reflect in me.

Not knowledge, but Thyself my joy, for this I pray.

We must read the Bible to know Him.

I was irregular in my daily devotions at first. But, through the years I have come to see the lifeline that simply reading the Bible is to His children. Everything I need is there—instruction, wisdom, perspective, power, prevention from sin, comfort and encouragement, fellowship with Jesus, the words to share with others.

Paul reminds us that it is profitable for "teaching *(showing us the path)*, reproof *(showing us when we get off the path)*, correction *(showing us how to get back on the path)*, and training in righteousness *(showing us how to stay on the path)*, so that the man of God will be adequate, equipped for every good work" (2 Timothy 3:16-17 *additional descriptions learned from Rick Warren*).

the cumulative effect of God's Word

It was in my fifties that I began to realize something amazing. Large deposits of Scripture were accumulating in my heart. I began to have the ability, by God's grace, to pull from this reservoir for myself and for others, as I ministered. As a pastor, sermon preparation became quicker, understanding deeper.

Such a cumulative effect is the product of what one man calls, "A long obedience in the same direction." The payoff is beyond description.

It makes me want to go pick up my Bible right now. I know the Lord is waiting there.

chapter 5

in which I was overwhelmed by the

Manifest Presence

ATMOSPHERE MATTERS. Try taking a long walk in muggy, downtown Houston versus a mountain stroll by a rushing stream in the Colorado Rockies. The environment changes everything.

The atmosphere of my fledgling spiritual journey was the Jesus Movement of the early 70's. Some refer to this as the fourth Great Awakening in America. Others would not go that far, believing that this mighty wind of God's Spirit was cut short in its effect, primarily because the churches would not change their traditional methods to accommodate the fresh movement of God.

"We're not gonna' let those hippies in here with their guitars!" they proudly declared as they quenched the Spirit. A very real lesson I would never forget.

The reality is this: more students came to Christ and were set on fire spiritually in the early 70's than any period in the last 100 years.

This was my birthing ground. I didn't know it. I just thought what was happening around me was normal. But I am so grateful.

Its ignition point was at Asbury College in Wilmore, Kentucky, on February 3, 1970. A simple chapel service, scheduled for one hour, lasted 24 hours a day for seven days. Teams from that movement went across the country and everywhere they testified, revival broke out. It became national news. People from all over the country went to see what was happening.

And it spread. College campuses exploded with God's presence. Even a college basketball game stopped at halftime for testimonies and never resumed play.

In San Antonio, a man who would become one of my greatest mentors, Manley Beasley, was speaking in Castle Hills Baptist Church. The Lord came in power, and that meeting, scheduled for a week, lasted a month. The effects lasted for years.

Jack Taylor, the pastor of Castle Hills, came to speak at our chapel service at Ouachita Baptist University in Arkansas. I was a freshman. A group of us had heard of what was happening around the country and were praying for God's outpouring on our campus. I was spellbound as he told the story of God's movement.

revival at noonday

As God would have it, I was leading our 15-minute, student-led noonday service. I asked Jack if he would walk across the campus and speak to us in Berry Chapel. He spoke for ten minutes.

And God came.

Spontaneously, but wonderfully directed by an Unseen Hand, students began to stand and humbly confess their need for Christ. Others repented, brokenheartedly, of their sin. Students came to genuine faith in Christ and were instantly changed. Many went to those they had hurt to clear their conscience. Some left the small chapel to find professors and confess the cheating they had done in their classes, or call parents to get things right.

Word began to spread and students filled the chapel. Classes across the campus were canceled. Students were sitting in the window frames and down the aisles on the floor. The 15-minute serviced lasted for over three hours.

It was the manifest presence of God.

The word "manifest" means, "clear, visible, unmistakable." God is always present, but there are moments when He chooses to reveal Himself in more visible ways ... when God "rends the heavens and comes down" to bring needed course corrections to a life, a church, a nation.

These seasons are very different than the normal work of the church. Jonathan Edwards of the First Great Awakening said that, in such times, the work of God is accelerated.

I saw it with my own eyes—felt it with my own spirit. More can happen in five minutes of God's manifest presence than 50 years of our best human effort.

"taste and see"

... the Psalmist said. It's the difference between riding a rickety bicycle by your own strength and being carried by a supersonic jet. Once you have been in the atmosphere of God's manifest presence, you long for it the rest of your life.

This doesn't mean you don't continue the normal, daily work of the Christian life and the building of the church. The routine of God's work moves on as God enlarges and develops His church, crashing through the gates of this world's kingdom—building a new Kingdom that will never end.

But, at every turn of this work, you are looking and praying for His greater manifestation and the rapid expansion of His kingdom that it brings.

It has driven me for 50 years, making me a student of the history of revival across the world. By God's grace, I have been in many moments and extended seasons where God has chosen to make Himself more greatly known.

It happened where I pastored in Norman, Oklahoma, when a two-week scheduled church meeting went into a third and fourth week, transforming the church for years to come.

He gloriously interrupted a normal worship service in 2011 in Little Rock at The Summit Church, visiting us in power. Halfway through my message, God told me to stop. And when I did, a man spontaneously stood and began to exhort us to listen to what was said and not to quench the moving of God's Spirit. The regular, one-hour worship service extended for over four hours. And the next night we came back and the service lasted four hours again.

We continued to meet every night except Saturday for *five weeks*. It drove us deep in prayer and broad in witness. Dozens and dozens of people were saved in short, dramatic fashion. People were baptized every night. Families were redeemed. Lives changed. Generosity exploded until there was "no more need" in the church.

I stood one night and read Acts 2:42-47, realizing that everything we observed and longed for in the first days of the church was happening among us in power in those days.

It was here, also, that I learned the incredible power of unceasing prayer. For most, prayer is a side-room, an appendage. God desires prayer to be the foundation. We are to live in the atmosphere of continual communion with God all day long.

During this season of revival, we were so interested in maintaining God's manifest presence that we prayed all day long. We were seeking to hear Him about everything so it demanded that we pray about everything! I had been puzzled for years by the command to "Pray without ceasing" (1 Thessalonians 5:17), but during these days I realized it was possible. And, that it is the foundational means of remaining in a right relationship with God.

And we've never been the same.

Oh, that You would rend the heavens and come down, That the
mountains might quake at Your presence—as fire kindles the
brushwood, as fire causes water to boil—to make Your name known
to Your adversaries, that the nations may tremble at Your presence!
When You did awesome things which we did not expect.
(Isaiah 64:1-3)

Something happened to me on that 1970 fall day in Berry Chapel as we encountered God. I have lived since then to cultivate the ground and prepare the soil wherever I am, so that God would be pleased to come in power. I want to remove any barriers to His presence. Every Sunday, and most days in-between, I'm expecting Him.

It explains my interest in the history and experience of God's great movements of revival and spiritual awakenings. It is one of God's ways—to periodically open heaven and manifest Himself in stunning brilliance—in a life, a church, a city, a nation. Only these moments can reset us, reminding us of His sovereign, Kingdom rule and rapidly advancing His kingdom.

His manifest presence is worth pursuing the rest of your life. And, one day soon, His followers will experience it with no end.

chapter 6

in which I was enrolled in the

school of faith

IT WAS TIME. My fiancé, Holly, and I had been engaged way too long. As we prayed about it, we sensed that God wanted us to get married the summer after our Junior year in college. We set the date with joy!

I remembered reading in the Bible that a man who doesn't provide for his household is "worse than an unbeliever," so I went to my dorm room to develop a budget. I'm no financial wizard, but on my $75 a week student pastorate salary, paying my way through college, I realized that we would just barely meet our budget. But then I realized I had included no money for food. We would be fine, if we just wouldn't eat for about a year!

I called Holly. "Honey, we can't get married. We'll have to delay the date. I can't provide!"

We both moaned. I went back from the hall phone to my room and opened my Bible to read my daily passage, which just happened to be in 1 Timothy, Chapter 6. God spoke His word to me, lifting it from the page right to my heart and our need.

> *"Instruct those who are rich in this present world not to be conceited or to fix their hope on the uncertainty of riches;*
> **but fix your hope on God, who will richly supply you**

with all things to enjoy." *(1 Timothy 6:17, emphasis mine)*

I raced back to the phone. "We're getting married," I cried. "God is going to give us all things to enjoy!"

We got married as planned and He provided as promised. Our first lesson, as a couple, in the School of Faith.

bean city

We were down to one can of baked beans. Literally. Holly and I had headed to seminary in Ft. Worth, Texas. She landed a Speech Therapist job in the Grand Prairie School District, but it was not enough for us to live on. I was looking for a church to pastor, along with the other 4,000 seminary students!

About two months in, it was Bean City. We gave a passing thought to calling our parents. But they couldn't get us money quick enough. And if God was God, wouldn't He provide? And so, we prayed, claiming the promise He had given us before our marriage.

I was walking to my first class on the next morning and will never forget the spot. Bo Brantley, a fellow student, met me at the top of the stairs by the Theology building.

"Bill, I'm glad I ran into you. Last night my wife and I felt strongly impressed that we were to give this to you." He handed me an envelope, patted my back, and walked away.

I ripped it open and was stunned to see four $100 bills! This was 1974! It was a million dollars!

We had a real need. We trusted God. He supplied. One of thousands of lessons.

God's operating principle

God has His ways, just like you have yours. The means by which everything functions in His Kingdom is by faith and faith alone. And He has designed a way for us to live in deepening dependency upon Him.

But faith is not a leap into the dark. It is stepping out on the revealed Word of God. God gives us instruction and promises in His Word. We must decide if we will trust Him. When we do, we will always find Him faithful.

A mentor to my father, and to me, was E.F. "Preacher" Hallock, who pastored in Norman, Oklahoma, for 46 years. "Preacher" had learned to live by the promises of God, and he taught my parents to do the same. And my father taught me.

There are 7,000 promises in the Bible. My current Bible has 1,000 pages which means there is an average of seven promises per page! Obviously, this is God's operating system and His means of developing faith. He gives us a promise for our situation, we are called to believe, and when we do He is always faithful. In this faith-process, we become more and more like Him.

For by these He has granted to us His precious and magnificent
promises, so that by them you may become partakers of the divine
nature, having escaped the corruption that is in the world by lust.
(2 Peter 1:4)

---

the purpose of the exercise

I had the privilege of pastoring a wonderful church plant in seminary, a mission of First Baptist Church in Dallas. In May, after my graduation, we had our first pulpit committee come from another church, asking us if we could come be their pastor. We were honored.

And then, another one came the next week. And another the next. In fact, if I remember, nine churches came in three months. They all told us they believed it was God's will for us to come pastor their church. Obviously, at least eight were wrong! We had a lot of important decisions to make.

The first committee was honoring. By about the fourth, it was nerve-wracking. My brother, Tom, called me one night. Tom was my other discipler in life, particularly at this season. He would call me on Saturday night to see if I had a sermon for Sunday. If not, he would give me about a dozen sermons!

"How are you doing, Bill?"

"I'm miserable, Tom. Holly and I have all these life-changing decisions to make and we're confused."

"This is not about those decisions," Tom calmly said. "God is trying to help you decide what the final authority is going to be for your life. You are deciding how you will decide. Will you live by mere logic, or are you going to live by faith in 'every word that proceeds from the mouth of God?' Are you going to search

God's Word, get a promise from Him, and proceed in faith, or just figure this out on your own?'"

There have been times in my life when God has changed me in five minutes of a sermon, a conversation, a prayer. This was one of those times.

babies, budgets & building the kingdom

It is critical that we learn God's operating principle. It has shaped my life for fifty years. It has determined for Holly and me how many children we would eventually have, (we ended up with eight on earth and two in heaven!), how we would handle our finances, how we would pastor, how we would live. And God has always been faithful. I could tell you hundreds and hundreds of stories.

I often tell my kids as they call me for counsel: "Well, you know what God is doing in this situation, right? He's helping you decide what will be the final authority for your life. The issue is not the issue. This is about faith. It always is. God is orchestrating experiences to teach you to search His Word, find His promises to you, and depend upon Him."

It's the most extraordinary way to live and our training for eternity. God is building men and women who will operate by His faith-system, as we will do forever in His eternal kingdom work.

The more you learn to trust Him the greater your experience of Him. And the greater your experience, the more you will fall in love with our promise-keeping God.

chapter 7

in which I was awed by

God-initiation

THERE WERE VERY FEW MEN that intimidated and intrigued me more. Manley Beasley was an itinerant preacher. At age 39 he had contracted six diseases, three of which were life threatening. For the next 20 years, he lived in incredible pain. But these years were his most powerful and productive as he traveled from church to church, bringing life out of death by faith.

These were the years I was privileged to know him.

In college, I heard that Manley was preaching at the same camp in Siloam Springs, Arkansas, where God had called me to preach years earlier. I got in my car and drove three hours just to hear him. He preached on living your whole life to lead people to Christ. His unusual style of preaching was confusing at first. Multiple streams that did not seem to connect ... until an explosion in your spirit in the end.

After the service, I got in my car to drive home and wept for three hours. The Word of God, coming through a man of God, had its effect on me.

I invited Manley to every church I pastored until his death. He became another mentor to me as he was to many, many young pastors.

a life-altering lunch

I was in such awe of Manley in the early years that I listened carefully to what he had to say. During one lunch in Harrah, Oklahoma, where I was pastor, Manley leaned across the table and said something that changed my life.

"Bill, the mark of a godly man is that everything he does is God-initiated." And then he stared at me for a moment (for effect I'm sure) and went back to his meal.

By no coincidence, my daily Scripture readings that week were in the Gospel of John. In Chapters 5-12, Jesus uses the word "initiation" six times (as translated in my New American Standard version) as He describes how He operated on earth (John 5:30; 8:28, 42; 12:49; 14:10; 16:13).

"I do nothing on my own initiative, but I speak these things as the Father taught Me," He said.
(John 8:28b)

This explained Christ to me. When He came in human flesh, Christ laid aside all His God-powers, choosing to live as a man so He could be the perfect sacrifice for our sin. But how, as a man, could He live perfectly? Never sin? Do miracles? Bring in the Father's kingdom?

It was all by God's initiation. Whatever He saw His father do, that's what He did, in the power of the Spirit who lived within Him. Whatever His Father said, those were the words that came through the man, Jesus. In so doing, He was not only showing us the Father, but showing us how we must live.

I realized this was why Jesus was constantly in prayer. Not only did He enjoy His Father in perfect love, but this communion gave Him direction. The Father was telling Him what to do, what to say, where to go. And Jesus simply moved in aggressive cooperation with the One He loved and lived to please. Since He had the Spirit in full measure, He was equipped to do whatever God instructed.

I began to long to live like this and help others do the same. Although I have lived by God-initiation very imperfectly, it has been my pursuit these last decades. In the churches I've had the privilege of pastoring, the constant question among us is not merely "Will this work?" but, "Does God seem to be initiating this?"

What if every believer was listening so closely to God's Spirit that we all did only what God initiated? What if churches moved like this? Not pulled by popular opinion or political wrangling, or even some preacher's best, humanistic ideas, but simply looking into heaven, seeing what the Father was doing, and following in the power of the Spirit?

The world would see God ... and His Kingdom would come.

life in two worlds

Paul would later encourage us further in this radical lifestyle with a powerful insight into where we really live.

> Therefore, if you have been raised up with Christ, keep seeking the things above, where Christ is, seated at the right hand of God. Set your mind on the things above, not on the things that are on earth. For you have died and your life is hidden with Christ in God. When Christ, who is our life, is revealed, then you also will be revealed with Him in glory. (Colossians 3:1-4)

If we have become believers in Jesus, we have been born anew into a spiritual Kingdom. This realm is just as real as the earthly world we inhabit, though unseen. We are seated, right now, in this heavenly place with Christ, but living physically in this world for a season. We live in both worlds and have access to both. A physical and spiritual matrix.

Paul tells us to keep our minds constantly fixed on the new Kingdom. We can dial in, through prayer and the Word of God, and see what the Father is initiating, what He wants. As we do, we can cooperate with God in seeing His "kingdom come and will be done on earth as it is being done in heaven" (Matthew 6:10). We can be Christ's agents to bring heaven to earth.

Wouldn't it be something if, at the end of your life, people would say about you, "I don't know quite what it was, but everywhere he/she was, the Kingdom of God seemed to come!"

This was how Christ lived and how we can live. And it changes everything.

chapter 8

in which I was crushed by pride

and lifted by brokenness

I THOUGHT I was a bigshot. The church I was pastoring in Norman, Oklahoma, in the 80's was exploding. We had doubled in size in three years. Our college ministry had grown from 25 students to over 350 hot-hearted believers from the University of Oklahoma. We saw 70 college students baptized in one year. Every year, we would send 100 students across the world in ministry. At one point, we had 22 students in seminary. (Notice how well I remember those numbers?)

I understood, somewhat, the nature of pride and fought it often. But I was slowly losing the battle.

In the midst of this wonderful growth, there were problems. An "old guard" contingent in the church was fighting against this expansion. "Their" church was not the same. The parking lot was full, the halls crowded. We had expanded to three Sunday morning worship services. Why, if you weren't careful, somebody would even take your seat!

Some of the men were losing the positions they had held for years (rightfully so), as God was raising the bar on leadership. So, they began to fight our leadership and direction. Pretty viciously, I might add. I had death threats.

We needed God.

My brother, Tom, told me about a group that had recently come to his church in Colorado. Life Action Ministries, led by Del Fehsenfeld, Jr., was a unique ministry. Completely devoted to seeing spiritual revival come to individuals, families, and churches, they would not come for less than two weeks to a church. They brought an entire team of children, youth, and worship leaders and two preachers.

We needed them. We needed God. I needed God.

front row seat

We arranged for them to come, and cleared the schedule so nothing would interfere. I decided to sit on the front row during the meeting, asking the Lord to bring revival to me first.

God began to move mightily. Fifty people came to Christ, with no evangelistic message preached. In their car, their shower, on the way to work—spontaneously captured by the love of God.

God confronted and removed piles of sin: anger, bitterness, unforgiveness, stealing, dishonesty. One night, over 400 people got up in ten minutes and moved to a prayer room to confess and deal with moral impurity. God had come and He was changing everything.

Halfway through the second week, the Lord sat down by me on the front row.

"Okay, son," He said. "It's time."

I waited in anticipation as He began to speak in the way only God can communicate to the human heart.

"Do you know why you love to hear people praise you so much? It's pride."

"Do you know why you get angered at your wife when she doesn't tell you on the way home from church what a great message you preached? Pride."

"Do you understand, my son, why you run from confrontation, always longing for everyone to like you? Why you have been hindered by a man-fearing, man-pleasing spirit? Pride, pride, pride."

"Do you understand why you won't let anyone finish a sentence, so you can tell your story, which you think is more important? Pride."

"Do you realize that you are overly concerned for numbers, not for My sake, but yours? That's pride."

He went on and on, revealing the groundwork of my heart. I have never been so lovingly, but fully reproved. Somehow, in the midst of that conversation, I fell to my knees while Del was preaching. And then to my face, sobbing into the carpet.

the mother of all sin

... is pride. Every bad thing you can think of flows from this deadly fountain. God hates pride, because He loves His creation and knows that a proud man has assumed a position that is reserved for God alone. Nothing about this is right.

God is opposed to the proud, but gives grace to the humble.

(James 4:6)

Think of being opposed by a 350-pound, professional tackle for a full 60 minutes on a football playing field. No fun. But think of getting up tomorrow morning—ready to raise your family, do your work, live your life—and you look across the line and God Himself is opposing you!

"Lord, why would you resist me? I thought you were on my side?"

"Son, I do love you and that's why I must oppose the direction you're headed. I have not given up on the possibility of helping you see that you cannot live for your own glory. If you will humble yourself—admitting your sin and acknowledging your need—I will pour out my enabling grace on you."

the beauty of brokenness

The recognition of the depth of my pride was designed by God to lead me somewhere, not to crush me. He was helping me see my need so greatly that I would gladly bow before Him in deepened brokenness and surrender.

Jesus said that this was the way we enter and thrive in His kingdom. In His most comprehensive sermon, He begins with the progressive components of the Beatitudes, each one building on the other:

Blessed are the poor in Spirit [those who see their need]
Blessed are those who mourn [over their sin and need]
Blessed are the meek [who, seeing their need, submit to the rule of the
King]
(Matthew 5:3-5, additions mine)

G. Campbell Morgan said that meekness is "the willingness to be governed by another." But we will never be willing to bend to Christ's authority if we have not seen our need profoundly. God must show us our pride, helping us along to humility. He must do it in such ways that we mourn and are anxious to surrender our will to His, which is true, spiritual brokenness. Until then, we think we can handle life on our own.

We could paraphrase these truths with one sentence:

Blessed is the man who sees his need so greatly
that he gladly bows.

Like a horse that has been broken, we must submit our will to the will of the Father. Until then, we are headstrong— unwilling and unusable.

the gift that keeps on giving

It's never "once and done" with pride. You will deal with it the rest of your life (or, at least, I have). Augustine said that just about the time he would think he had overcome pride, the devil would whisper in his ear, "Your brother has become the bishop of Alexandria!"

But it is a glorious thing when God shows you your pride, as He did to me on that carpet (and has many, many times since). When you begin to see its nature. When you start to abhor it as He does. When you recognize it more quickly and repent more fully.

And it is even more glorious when you begin to enter what Tim Keller describes as "The Freedom of Self-Forgetfulness."

> "Gospel-humility is not needing to think about my-self. Not needing to connect things with myself. It is an end to thoughts such as, 'I'm in this room with these people, does that make me look good? Do I want to be here?' True gospel-humility means I stop connecting every experience, every conversa-tion, with myself. In fact, I stop thinking about my-

self. The freedom of self-forgetfulness. The blessed rest that only self-forgetfulness brings."

C.S. Lewis said, "Humility is not thinking less of yourself, but thinking of yourself less." It is being so consumed with God and others that you don't even think about yourself at all. What freedom!

a fresh lesson in the hallway

I was walking through the church one Sunday recently. One of our other pastors was preaching, and for some reason (maybe we'll call it ... pride?), I felt a little bit on the edges. I wasn't involved in leading this Sunday. Also, I wasn't sure the other pastor was handling the text quite right (the way I would have preached it!) And to top it off, I was not well physically and was in a general grouch!

The Lord never misses a training opportunity like this. He gently whispered in my ear, "Bill, it's not about you today ... or any day."

Oh, my.

I realized my sin and repented, grateful to be serving the great God who loves me enough, and knows me well enough, to show me the hidden recesses of my heart. To keep me from stealing glory from the One to whom alone it is due. To remind me that I am a small, but useful player in His big Kingdom plan.

I've never quite gotten over that night on the carpet. I pray I never will.

chapter 9

in which we learned

God's sufficiency in suffering

"HE'LL NEVER WALK," the doctor at the Children's Hospital in Oklahoma City said. "You need to get ready for this."

We weren't prepared for this news with the birth of our first-born son, David. He came into the world both feet first and the umbilical cord had been constricted and oxygen flow interrupted. The doctor literally yanked him into the world. We later discovered that this moment had caused the nerves to be severed from his spine to his right leg.

seasons

Just as God has designed summer, winter, spring, and fall for unique purposes, so God designs seasons of our lives. And each season has its purpose.

The 1980's, for Holly and me, were a time of great joy and growth coupled with fairly intense suffering such as we had never known. It was the season to learn of God's sufficiency in all things.

Holly and I were in our early 30's. Many glorious things happened, but also many hard things. But navigating those hard issues formed for us, by God's grace, an understanding of His sufficiency and sovereignty like nothing else. I wouldn't have chosen these moments, but I wouldn't trade them.

The joy of our time in Norman, Oklahoma, was the growth of the church (Trinity Baptist), the numbers of people who came to Christ, the hundreds of people who were discipled, the ministry to many students at the University of Oklahoma, and our deep and rich friendships. Of particular joy to me was the development of 100 men—our Shepherd's School, we called it—into a strong band of godly, equipped leaders. These men would lead us, as a church, through a vital transition and beyond.

Personally though, we faced a lot of "stuff." In a period of five years, Holly and I dealt with ...

- The miscarriage of two children.

- The difficult birth of our first son, who, they told us, would never walk.

- Multiple staff members I had inherited with multiple tough issues. One was discovered with a serious sexual problem and had to be released. Another Children's intern was discovered to be a child molester. (This ended up on the front page of the state paper two Sundays in a row and the topic of the top radio talk show.) He later went to prison.

- The dramatic moral fall of my pastor father, who ultimately left my mother— the most devastating issue I'd ever faced.

- My mother's rapid regression into Alzheimer's and our caring for her the final three years of her life.

- An all-out battle for the soul of the church over the authority of Scripture and its place in our church. This occurred because of a bitter leader who lost his control of the church and then gathered people to oppose what was happening and fire me. A two-year battle ended in a 5-hour business meeting as we disciplined him from the church. 200 people left the next Sunday.

Holly said to me one day, during that season, "I wish we could have one year in which we didn't have to say, 'Well ... that was different!'" Normalcy had gone out the window.

It seemed to be a continuously hard season. Where was God in all of this?

hearing His voice

No one realizes the value of developed spiritual disciplines until they are most needed. By the grace of God, He had built into me the regular, daily study of His Word and the practice of prayer. Early morning is my best time to meet with Him. God had graciously revealed Himself to me in these hours, year after year. I have said, with genuine humility and gratitude, "By God's grace, I know how to find Him."

Therefore, let everyone who is godly pray to You in a time when You may be found; surely in a flood of great waters they will not reach him.
(Psalm 32:6)

There is an art to hearing God. It does not happen overnight.

Let's say we put a blindfold on you, placed 100 women in front of you, and one of them was your mother. Then we asked them each to call your name. When your mother called your name, you would recognize her. Instantly. The reason? Years of time and conversation. You know her voice.

There are many competing voices around us. To be able to discern the still, small voice of God takes time in His presence.

When it becomes discernible to the seeking heart, it becomes the most important Voice in the world. But if you never learn to hear God in the quietness, you will find it harder to find Him in the storm.

What carried me in this season was God's promises and direction to my heart, every day, through His Word and prayer. Day after day, He would give me a fresh promise that would carry me until the next, needed installment. This happened hundreds of times. I have journals filled with His instructions.

When I was being opposed:

- *He who digs a pit will fall into it, and he who rolls a stone, it will come back on him. (Proverbs 26:27)*

- *An evil man will be ensnared by the transgression of his lips. (Proverbs 12:13)*

- *Do not answer a fool according to his folly, or you will also be like him. (Proverbs 26:4)*

- *If possible, so far as it depends on you, be at peace with all men. Never take your own revenge, beloved, but leave room for the* wrath of God, for it is written, "Vengeance is Mine, I will repay," says the Lord. "But if your enemy is hungry, feed him, and if he is thirsty, give him a drink; for in so doing you will heap burning coals on his head." Do not be overcome by evil, but overcome evil with good. (Romans 12:18-21)

- As for you, you meant evil against me, but God meant it for good in order to bring about this present result, to preserve many people alive. (Genesis 50:20)

When I was dealing with tough staffing issues:

- "An elder must be above reproach" (1 Timothy 3:2)

- "Do not receive an accusation against an elder except on the basis of two or three witnesses." (1 Timothy 5:19)

When my father fell

- Forgive each other, just as God, in Christ, has forgiven you. (Ephesians 4:32)

- "Because he has loved Me, therefore I will deliver him; I will set him securely on high, because he has known My name. He will *call upon Me, and I will answer him; I will be with him in trouble. I will rescue him and honor him. With a long life I will satisfy him and let him see My salvation." (Psalm 91:14-16)*

When my mother was fearful in her Alzheimer's:

- *"For such is God, our God forever and ever. He will guide me until death." (Psalm 48:14)*

Over and over, day after day, God spoke. I have journals filled with hundreds of verses, directly applied to my need. I would find myself climbing up on His promises and sitting down each day in faith. It was what carried me; the only antidote for my anxious heart. I had all I needed, when I needed it. And, EVERY PROMISE CAME TRUE!

Holly and I discovered a depth of God's sovereignty that one can only realize in suffering. It made us love Him all the more, for He is faithful. Always. Completely. Sufficiently. He is never in a hurry ... but always right on time. **And by the way ...**

- My son's leg was miraculously healed as the nerves some-how reattached or were re-innervated. He's a strapping man with four kids, planting a church in Seattle ... walking and serving by the faithfulness of God.

- Even with our two miscarriages, God gave us a total of 10 kids! We look forward to meeting the 2 children that we had the privilege of conceiving by God's creative power, but never knew, in heaven someday soon.

- The church in Norman, Oklahoma, came through those days and continued to grow into a wonderful, powerful fellowship. That experience equipped me as no other and, I trust in some measure, is now helping other pastors as I counsel them.

- My father repented, returned to the Lord, and lived a grateful, humble, useful life till he died at age 97.

- And my mother was translated into the glorious presence of God and is enjoying Him—face to face—with a perfect mind.

And He has said to me, "My grace is sufficient for you, for power is perfected in weakness." Most gladly, therefore, I will rather boast about my weaknesses, so that the power of Christ may dwell in me. Therefore, I am well content with weaknesses, with insults, with distresses, with persecutions, with difficulties, for Christ's sake; for when I am weak, then I am strong.

(2 Corinthians 12:9-10)

chapter 10

in which I learned

the freedom of forgiveness

SOMETHING WAS TERRIBLY WRONG. It had been a joy to pastor in the same metropolitan area with my dad. I was in Norman, Oklahoma, and he was the Director over 160 churches in Oklahoma City. God had mightily used my dad. In fact, as he came to the final year of his retirement he was recognized as the top city leader in our denomination in all of America.

But in the next year, I watched a creeping darkness come over his soul. Depression settled in like the morning fog. He rarely looked me in the eye. Closest of friends and my greatest counselor, he now seemed a million miles away.

My brother, Tom, and I both noticed this change. "If I didn't know better," Tom said, "I'd think dad was having an affair. He has all the signs." But we both knew this could not possibly be true.

As our concern grew, I called one of his co-workers. "Ed, is there anything going on that you've noticed with my dad? Something seems wrong," I said.

There was a long pause. Then weeping. "We need to talk," Ed sadly replied.

The next day we met in a coffee shop and Ed disclosed to me the signs he was seeing. Dad was involved with a lady at his office.

A few weeks later, my brothers and my sister all came, unannounced, to my mom and dad's house and confronted him. He denied any problem. We wept and prayed and pleaded, and then began a two-year roller coaster of pain. Dad lied and left and returned, and repeated the cycle. He lived in darkness and denial. One day he left and didn't come back, divorcing my precious mom and marrying another.

a lesson I didn't want to learn

It blindsided me. My dad would later say, "No man can rise so high that he cannot fall," but it seemed surreal in my father's case. Everything I had learned about moral purity, I'd learned from him. Most of my theology and practical Christianity had been learned at his feet.

I was overwhelmed. Stunned. And mad.

It grew during the two years when dad was home and involved in the affair and denial, but I still held on to hope. After he left, bitterness took root in my soul and I didn't know it. I felt numb and not very interested in my Bible or prayer, for I wasn't really interested in what God had to say. I hate to write those words, but it was true. I felt God had let us down.

God under a cottonwood

When you are bitter, your kids seem to get louder, and you become agitated at minor disturbances! One night I was particularly on edge and I told my wife I was going for a walk. I was less than a block away when I stopped under a huge cottonwood tree in our neighborhood.

For years, I had prayed a deep, sincere prayer: "God, whatever you need to do to make me a man of God, please do it!" And I meant it.

I stood under that cottonwood, paralyzed in my tracks. Looking up at God, I lifted my fist and said out loud, "Lord, if this is what it takes to make me a man of God, I don't want it!"

I was shocked as the words burst out of my soul.

God wasn't. He knew where I was. And then, in the most gracious way I'd ever experienced, God began to minister to me under that tree.

"Son, I didn't cause this sin. I'm not responsible for evil. I came to deliver you in times just like this. You are upset with me for allowing this to happen in your family ... and you're holding me at arm's length. I'm the only One who can help you and yet, in your blaming of Me, you are shutting out the very One who is your greatest Advocate."

In a few minutes that seemed like an hour, the Spirit of God washed over my soul. I began to weep greatly and repent deeply. "I am so sorry, Lord." And I opened my fists.

I had been saying to God, "God, I will not receive this in my life!" which was foolish. It was already in my life. But in that moment, I relaxed my hands and said, "Lord, I will receive this issue in my life, as if it is from You. And I know that You will faithfully weave it together for good in the tapestry of our lives."

I was embracing the sovereignty of God. And the acceptance of the circumstance opened the way for the most important step: forgiveness.

a new definition

... of forgiveness began to grow in my life. I now remind people that ...

Forgiveness is my responsibility

as a choice of my will,

made possible by God's grace,

to release a debt,

by faith,

for the glory of God.

Read that definition again—slowly, carefully. It's a little cumbersome, but each phrase is very important.

Forgiveness is ...

- **My responsibility:** Regardless of what others have done, I am responsible for the sin of my unforgiveness.

- **As a choice of my will made possible by God's grace:** It is not an act of my emotions, but a choice I can always make because of the sufficiency of God's empowering grace.

- **To release a debt:** The reason I am holding this in the ledger book of my heart is to make others pay (in multiple ways). Forgiveness transfers this issue from my courtroom to God's, believing that He is fully capable of taking care of others.

- **For the glory of God:** There is nothing that illustrates God more clearly and shows others the remarkable power of God to help us through the deepest hurts of life than forgiveness.

We think people owe us things. "He doesn't have a right to treat me that way, to do (this or that.)" We become upset with them, and ultimately God, because we think we deserve better.

The truth is, we deserve hell. Every good thing we have in this life, including our eternal forgiveness, has come by the kind intervention of a forgiving Father. When we realize how much He has forgiven us, we are able to release the debt we're holding against others ... a debt in which we have been demanding payment.

Forgive each other, just as God, in Christ has forgiven you.
(Ephesians 4:33)

My mother was the greatest forgiver in this whole moment. Her forgiveness helped me to forgive not only my dad, but the lady he married.

one step further

After several years of Alzheimer's digression, my mother suffered a cerebral hemorrhage and went into the hospital. What the doctor thought would only last for a few days until her death, lasted seven weeks in the Norman Regional hospital. Her room became a sanctuary of God's presence.

The greatest day came when she awakened about two weeks into this ordeal. She told my sister and me to "Forgive, forgive, forgive!" ... the only words we would be able to hear in her garbled speech. The next day my brothers and all our spouses gathered around her bed. It was, perhaps, the greatest worship service I'll ever experience this side of heaven.

And as we were there, my dad called.

He called to ask mom's forgiveness, the first conversation they had in two years. She mouthed words of forgiveness that she had practiced 1,000 times. My dad's repentance would prove deep and real. Both dad and his new wife had come to repentance.

the last layer of forgiveness

I forgave my dad's wife, but I didn't love her. Didn't even want to see her. They had moved far away and had been removed from our lives. One day, they were coming through Oklahoma and I realized I would see her. I didn't know what to do, but I asked the Lord to help me.

"Lord, you live inside of me. You ARE love. All the love I need is found in You and You are in me. I gladly give You my body. Would You love her through me?"

One of the greatest illustrations to me of the reality of Christ happened to me in the parking lot of a Holiday Inn in Clinton, Oklahoma. I got out of the car, saw her, and loved her. I threw my arms around her, expressing the love of God. And I have loved her since that day.

God redeemed them both ... *and me.*

Dad would later tell his story to thousands of young pastors. He would begin with this statement:

"No man is too high that he cannot fall,
and no man is too low that he cannot rise again
by the grace of God."

You won't make it through this world without bitterness if you don't learn how to forgive. Forgiveness is the lesson of the Bible, from Genesis to Revelation. God, who is relentlessly interested in our development, allows circumstances in our lives to bring us to this liberating truth.

You can forgive and love anyone who has done anything. It is a gift made possible by the enabling grace of God and the powerful presence of His Spirit within you.

Why is He so interested in teaching us how to forgive and love those who hurt us? It's because you are never more like Jesus than when you forgive.

chapter 11

in which I began to understand

why I am here

SIX OF US SAT IN A LIVING ROOM overlooking the Arkansas River in October of 1998. These men had taken a bold step. They left their secure jobs and salaries to plant a church they had dreamed about for many years. There in that living room, I had the privilege of giving the first dollar bill, which was our church budget for the first seven days! Along with our wives and children, we committed ourselves to Christ and the work we believed He was calling us to begin.

We weren't sure how the church would do, knowing that we could all be selling shoes in a few months! But our hearts beat in unison about what the church should be.

We longed to be a part of a church that was a microcosmic picture of heaven, filled with the presence of God. A church that worshiped fervently, loved passionately, preached and followed God's Word authentically, shared Christ boldly, and was fueled by a clear understanding of our mission.

A community where anyone would be welcomed and accepted unconditionally, but helped to become all God designed them to be. Where gossip and conflict, rumor and fighting was non-existent, because we wanted to show the world what heaven is like. Where a culture of multiplying discipleship existed as we invested our lives in the lives of others—over and over again—to help as many as possible find the beauty of Jesus and the fullness of His purpose.

We longed to reach the next generation for Christ, and to train them so they could reach the generation behind them. To be a church that had in its DNA a passion for reaching children and students continually. A church that would take a risk on young leaders, knowing that they will be the leaders in the next decades. A church where the wisdom of older leaders was valued and shared and the zeal of young leaders was released and given wings.

A place that valued substance over style and transparency over a façade of religion. We wanted to embrace change as a value, so that no temporary wineskin would become permanent and binding—where we would be free to move instantly at the Spirit's prompting. Where strong leaders led in biblical unanimity and all surrendered their opinions to the initiations of Christ, who is the Head of the church.

A church that prayed with no intermission, believed God's Word with no qualifications, and followed Christ with no reservations.

And the crazy thing was, we were filled with absolute faith that it could happen.

growing up

We spread the word that we were beginning. At an interest meeting a week leader, we all wept as 130 people walked through the double doors into a school cafeteria, and The Summit Church began.

I have eight children (on earth) and many grandchildren. By the time you read this, there will be more grandchildren I am sure. And, if you happen to read this in a few years, the Elliff clan may be the size of small town!

One of the great joys of my life and Holly's is to watch them all grow. Their first steps, first words. Their immature affections. Their maturing understanding. The struggle of teen years and the rapid, apprenticing growth of young adulthood. And the exquisite beauty as they mature into the unique men and women, husbands and wives, fathers and mothers, disciples and disciplers that God had in mind when He first created them.

At each stage, another beautiful dimension is layered into their lives. One by one, and year by passing year, their lives get richer, fuller, and more productive.

God's kingdom and His kingdom communities (local churches) mature in much the same way. Paul said that God gives gifted men to aid in this spiritual growth.

> And He gave some as apostles, and some as prophets, and some as evangelists, and some as pastors and teachers, for the equipping of the saints for the work of service, to the **building up of the body of Christ;** until we all attain to the unity of the faith, and of the knowledge of the Son of God, **to a mature man, to the measure of the stature which belongs to the fullness of Christ.** (Ephesians 4:11-13, emphasis mine)

Over those first years, and increasingly now, I've watched something beautiful and healthy at The Summit Church, by God's grace. Like a child measured year by year on a doorframe, I've watched her grow up to look more and more like Jesus as He layers in what we need.

I remember when we learned to worship—seeing God as He is and giving Him what He deserves. And the season when God began to break our hearts for a lost world and started sending dozens, then hundreds of us all around the world.

Giant steps were taken in our understanding of revival as we began to pursue the manifest presence of Christ. And then, God came down, in five weeks of unplanned, uninterrupted glory. Those were the days we learned how to pray at an entirely new level ... when we realized you really could pray without ceasing and that prayer can do anything that God can do. That prayer is not to be a side-room, but the foundation of the church. And we've never been the same.

God has grown us up in our understanding of the kingdom, that it is bigger than one church or denomination. That there is an inherent spiritual power in the unified prayers and shoulder-to-shoulder steps of the whole church in the whole city with the whole gospel. He's taught us what can happen when the one church in the city unites and a spiritual light show erupts in ways a whole city can see.

I remember many unique moments when God increased our understanding of generosity, which is right at the center of His giving heart. I've watched us grow in dependency upon the Lord. We have begun to learn that faith is God's only operating system with His creation. He speaks about everything and we are called to listen and follow, confident of His faithfulness. We're cooperating with Him to create a sustained culture of personal evangelism. And on and on and on.

We're growing up, by the grace of God.

there's something irresistible

... about heaven. Imagine a world of perfect love, as Jonathan Edwards once preached. Imagine a kingdom where you love everyone perfectly, everyone loves you perfectly, you love God perfectly, and you are able to understand and finally rest deeply in His perfect love for you.

Where there is no sin or darkness. No conflict or war. No pain or sickness. Where you will be able to do exactly what you were created to do in fullness and power.

The kingdom of heaven is real, and when a humble man or woman submits to the rule of the King they are transferred from the "kingdom of darkness to the kingdom of God's dear Son" (Colossians 1:13). We literally become citizens of two completely real and accessible worlds—the physical earthly world and the spiritual, heavenly world. (Study Colossians 3:1-3 to see if this is not so.)

This is why we can become men and women who are able, through our union with Christ and cooperation with Him, to see "His kingdom come and His will be done on earth as it is (being done) in heaven" (Matthew 6:10). We are to help bring in the kingdom—in a life, a family, a city—and to bring people INTO that kingdom. And that's why the church exists.

so, it's very clear to me

... what my purpose is on this earth. I am to cooperate with God in developing multiplying disciples and multiplying communities of fully devoted followers of Jesus Christ. I am to work, under Christ's initiation, to see kingdom communities built that look like heaven. That carry the aroma of Christ. That are so irresistible that a man outside of God's kingdom will long to be a part.

I am to call people to unceasing prayer for revival and spiritual awakening, so the church can accelerate in revival seasons and expand even more rapidly. To do anything and everything possible to help the kingdom grow.

Jesus once said that the kingdom of heaven is like a pearl of great price or a treasure hidden in a field. If a man ever understands the value of that pearl or treasure, he will sell everything he has to possess it.

My purpose is to hold up the pearl ... in my life, my family, and the church in which I am a grateful member. I am to resist the intrusion of a fallen world in my life, replacing it with the glories of heaven, so that the difference of my life, and whatever church I am in, is like a fragrant aroma.

And the reason is simple for this determined, intentional life: He is worthy and people are needy.

Christ has done everything for me. I want others to see His worth and beauty, His power and glory, and the place He has prepared for us eternally. For to know Him is to have life, and to miss Him is eternal death and separation from all that matters and lasts.

Many men have their purposes for living, I'm sure. But I am overwhelmed with the majesty of my purpose and the weight of glory which drives me.

And I deeply believe that the purpose He has given me can (and should) be yours too. You may not be called to pastor a church, but you are designed to build God's kingdom—one life at a time, beginning with yours—until we grow up into Him.

chapter 12

in which I am

looking for MORE

IT WAS ONE OF those rare privileges. My brother, Jim, called and asked me if I would like to have J. Oswald Sanders in my church for a week. Sanders was in his mid-80's and a seasoned missionary statesman, having led Overseas Missionary Fellowship (which Hudson Taylor started in China) for many years. His books were enduring classics. He had outlived three wives.

(My favorite Sanders line he told me in private? "My second wife," he told me, "had the spiritual gift of deflation.")

Sanders had left his New Zealand home that year and traveled for ten straight months before coming to our church in Norman, Oklahoma. Over dinner the first night, he began to ask me questions. It was not the usual banter, but deep questions about life and ministry. I knew he was getting to know my heart.

But there was more. I began to sense he was asking questions to learn and grow. Each morning, he would hand me 10-15 handwritten letters to "put in the post" for him. I have one of those letters he sent to me, a cherished possession. And all week he preached on Caleb, who, in his later years said, "Give me that mountain." It was very evident: Sanders was still growing. This mighty man of God knew, and he taught me to see, that there is always …

more

That week left an eternal impact on me. Sanders was a man who believed that there was always another mountain ahead in the Christian life. That you could never exhaust the mind of God or the opportunities for ministry.

To me, this has become one of the things that gives meaning and purpose to every season of life. Each puddle has its purposes—each day its design. And, if I'm alert and listening, I can be thrilled right up to the last breath with the fullness of God.

There are thousands of lessons I have learned and thousands more ahead. The few that I've placed in this little story of my brief life are those which have particularly shaped me. Perhaps God will give me the grace to write another book years from now, with a few more lessons!

headed somewhere

What few of us seem to remember is that our brief life is merely a preface. How we respond to Christ's gracious claims upon our lives (which He created) determines what we will be doing in eternity. Those who follow Christ and are faithful in a few things, Jesus said, will be "put in charge" of much in His eternal kingdom (Matthew 25:21).

We will not be sitting on a cloud eating chocolates in heaven. It is a place of kingdoms, enterprise, administration, activity, and labor that is free from the curse of sin. I believe we will be doing the unique things that we were designed to do when we were in God's mind before He created us. Imagine the thrill of such a life!

When we look back on our earthly lives, we will see that God was moving and guiding, teaching and molding, preparing us for eternity.

grateful

If I were to die today, I would be overwhelmingly grateful for the life God has given me. The seasons He's allowed me to experience, my incredible heritage and fabulous family (especially my wife), the gracious opportunities, the rich experiences, each church I have served and the people I've pastored. Most of all, I am most awed by His compassionate intervention in my life and His self-disclosure. He has let me know HIM—and to know Him is life at its best.

If He lets me continue for another season on this earth, I am convinced there is more of God to experience and know. And certainly, hundreds of people that I could introduce to Him.

There's always *more.*

In His precise timing someday, I will shed this worn-out clothing and take up a new robe and new residence. I will enter a season that will never end, filled with inexhaustible glory and unending purpose. And, in the rarified air of eternity, I will thank Him continually, face to face, for the ...

large ways

of a **powerful** God,

taught to a **weak** creature

in his **brief** life,
preparing him for an **endless** eternity.

epilogue

Your Seasons

WHILE STUDYING THE life of King David recently, I discovered that David's life is summarized in the Bible in 12-15 events. We know David's life as it was shaped by these chapters, these seasons.

Everyone's life has these chapters. Some are seen as wonderful and helpful, while others are often viewed as hard and even damaging. But, seen through God's perspective, it is often the hardest seasons where we learn the most.

If you know God, (and the MORE you know God), you realize that nothing is ever wasted with Him. He takes even the toughest moments and "works it together for good" by His sovereign hand for those who are loving Him (Romans 8:28). If you're God, you can do things like that.

He is motivated by perfect love for all those who follow Him. And each season has a training attached. Although we rarely understand this, God is equipping us for life through each chapter. He knows that our greatest joy will come from being used to help others. And so, He trains us through all of life's experiences, equipping us to have something in our backpack to pull out at just the right moment to come alongside and lift the load of those in need.

Blessed be the God and Father of our Lord Jesus Christ, the Father of mercies and God of all comfort, who comforts us in all our affliction so that we will be able to comfort those who are in any affliction with the comfort with which we ourselves are comforted by God.

(2 Corinthians 1:3-4)

The older I get, the more I see my life through the lens of these seasons. And, I see others' lives like this as well. This is in part because God took me through an exercise one night of seeing my life this way, which led to the writing of this small book. Suddenly God's working in my life became very clear. C.S. Lewis talks about this clarity in *Mere Christianity.*

> Imagine yourself as a living house. God comes in to rebuild that house. At first, perhaps, you can understand what He is doing. He is getting the drains right and stopping the leaks in the roof and so on; you knew that those jobs needed doing and so you are not surprised. But presently He starts knocking the house about in a way that hurts abominably and does not seem to make any sense. What on earth is He up

to? The explanation is that He is building quite a different house from the one you thought of—throwing out a new wing here, putting on an extra floor there, running up towers, making courtyards. You thought you were being made into a decent little cottage: but He is building a palace. He intends to come and live in it Himself."

My prayer is these pages will help you see the moments of your life with greater clarity. Maybe there is some lesson He taught me that is right where you are ... something He is trying to say to you.

But the fullest measure of help might be if you would get a good cup of coffee, take a pen and paper (as I did one night) and ask the Lord to show you the lessons in each chapter of your life.

Ask Him this question: "Father, what have you been walking me through and what have You been teaching me at each season?" You will be shocked at how clear your life becomes to you. And, you will find yourself better equipped to be able to help others.

Who knows? He may want you to write it down to give to those around you. Remember ...

"When you have passed through enough puddles with Christ, you feel you have something to tell. Something that might help those who are coming behind. It's not really about you, but about Him. So, you begin to tell your tale."

other writings by bill elliff

~Books~

The Presence Centered Church

OneCry

A Nationwide Call for Spiritual Awakening

With Byron Paulus

Whitewater

Navigating the Rapids of Church Conflict

(Graceful Truth Series)

The Line of Faith

40 Days to Deepened Dependency

The Essential Presence

40 Days to Increased Intimacy with God

Prayer With No Intermission

40 days to Persevering Prayer

~Children's Books~

The Child of 10,000 Names

The Christmas Tree Story

Scott Edge with Bill Elliff

~Booklets~

Healing the Harbored Hurts of Your Heart

Lifting Life's Greatest Load

How to Gain and Maintain a Clear Conscience

Everyman

Raising MORE Kids Who Follow Christ

Holly Elliff with Bill Elliff

To order, go to our store at

www.billelliff.org

Made in the USA
Lexington, KY
26 October 2018